T0210211

ROOMS OF THE MIND

POEMS

MAKENZIE CAMPBELL

central
avenue
PUBLISHING

2021

*This one's for me. For all the spaces I've climbed out of. For all the
times I've learned to make my own light. For every last beat my
heart has made until I've reached this moment.*

This one is for me.

Published by Central Avenue Publishing, an imprint of Central Avenue Marketing Ltd.
www.centralavenuepublishing.com

ROOMS OF THE MIND

Trade Paperback: 978-1-77168-249-7
Epub: 978-1-77168-250-3
Mobi: 978-1-77168-251-0

Published in Canada
Printed in United States of America

1. POETRY / General   2. POETRY / Women Authors

10 9 8 7 6 5 4 3 2 1

We retreat into these rooms, our rooms of the mind, and burrow ourselves into their comfort. Sometimes we hide in a room of fear. We crouch ourselves into the smallest corner, cover our eyes with our hands, and wait for the danger to pass. Sometimes we hide in heartbreak, unsure of what to do with all this pain. We bask in love and all its beautiful fortunes. We rest in hope with our fingers crossed, wishing for goodness to come.

We all have rooms in our minds.

Some doors are locked and some ajar.

The question is: which will you choose to open today?

Trigger warning: some poems in this collection
reference alcohol use, sexual abuse, suicide
ideation and possibly other difficult topics.

Please proceed with this in mind and take
breaks or stop reading when needed.

xx Makenzie

CONTENTS

ROOMS OF THE MIND

ROOM #1 - IN LONELY

Lying here by the shore,
I hear the moonlight
kissing the water.

It sounds like loneliness.

It sounds like a feeling I'm all too familiar with.

I walk in and there's a river on the floor.

Someone who doesn't know what to do with their hands.

Empty bottles littering the carpet.

And when I look into his eyes,

I see something even emptier.

A sadness that has no end.

A sadness that comes from nowhere and everywhere all at once.

"Just give me something to point to. A reason for this ache. Give me something to call it."

I say, "Not all grievances have names. That's the hardest part."

crash into me

crash into me

swirl around my ankles

and take me to the deep

      i want to be one with the water

      i want to be one with the sand

      i want to be one with the silence

IT'S NIGHTS LIKE THESE
I MISS YOU MOST,
WHEN OUR MEMORIES
TURN INTO YOUR GHOSTS
AND HAUNT MY DREAMS
SO I CAN'T SLEEP.
HERE I LIE AWAKE
IN MY LONELY.

You have this way of letting words float out of your mouth
and materialize to rocks in my belly.

I am hoping Love finds me.

It's up to the universe now

because my fingers are tired of searching for four-leaf clovers

and I've given up on 11:11.

Shooting stars are no longer poetic and I don't bother to make wishes on them.

I've been actively searching for Love since I was fifteen.

After so many years you start to lose yourself.

You start to doubt yourself.

I started to hate myself.

Now I'm just tired.

She can find me when she's ready and I'll be here.

She knows I'll always be here.

I've dressed up my damage between these lines. I didn't mean to. I thought this was my release but the more I write, the more I feel married to the idea of my pain.

A comfort and a curse, to know a feeling so familiar. How sad it is to say I could choose to turn away, but time after time I seem to stay.

I always stay.

Reaching for you
      is like reaching for air
at the bottom of
      a swimming pool.
I'm weighted and drowning
      but still here trying
to grasp a hand that dances
      above the surface,
too afraid
      to dive in.

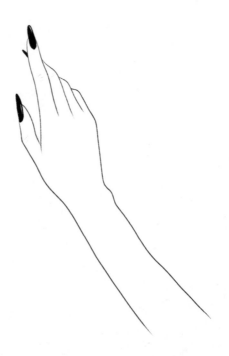

Before I met you

I had a lion within me.

I used to demand things I deserved

and protest in the face of injustice.

I had no fears except the one where I lost my roar.

And then I met you,

and a soft spot opened inside me.

My claws retracted.

My teeth turned dull.

And before I knew it,

you had tamed my wild into your average house cat.

What are house cats to do

when they are thrown out from their homes?

My lion would have survived your leaving.

I am more than the wars I've lost with myself,
      and there have been many.
It looks like:
      hiding in bed for days
      empty dinner plates
      responsibilities stacking like dirty laundry.
What do you do if the battle is in your homeland?
What do you defend if it's the one firing?

I throw up white flags and crown Anxiety the victor.
She smiles with all her teeth.

But this battle is only one of many.
And she is not always the one smiling.
There have been triumphs, small and large.
And every new day brings the possibility of renewal.
Of growth.
Of something beautiful.

I am more than the wars I've lost with myself.
I know because despite losing
      I am still here.
         I am here.
            I am here.

I guess my shirt must have been too low-cut or my lipstick
too alluring. I guess asking you to walk me home
made you think I owed you something.

It's my fault.

I should have dressed more conservatively, and I shouldn't
have accepted any drinks or asked you for help when
walking in a straight line was only feasible two hours
earlier.

I shouldn't have let you into my room (even though you
didn't ask) or let you take my clothes off (even though you
didn't hesitate) as I lay there silent on the floor. I should
have spoken up and said no. I should have fought off the
alcohol that led me to my hushed stupor.

Somehow it's my fault
        that my silence
        let you believe
        you could take advantage
        of my body.

I DON'T KNOW HOW TO NOT BE SAD

i don't know how to look at fruit and not think it sour
before sweet

i don't know how to look at my hands and not see them
empty

to look at the moon and not feel the lonely pool at my feet

to not wonder where you are among the stars

to not cast joy in a dark shadow

to be in summer and not wish for rain

to not brace for a storm that hasn't yet come

to not denounce happiness before it's begun

ROOM #2 - IN FEAR

A stranger in my own home.

I look in the mirror and find that she is gone.

Who I thought she was, she isn't,

who she wants to be, she's not.

Stuck in a sort of purgatory inside the walls of her skin.

Her movements are slowed by the weight of all the words she's been holding in.

Is it possible to feel heavy and vacant at the same time?

One look into her eyes and I sense her empty suffocation. How she wants to invite someone in, but fear consumes everything down to her fingertips.

She's lost in herself.

I always pray she finds her way out.

"what if"

    has me on a collared leash

You stood across from me in front of a closed, locked door.

Sweet words began to slither out of your mouth, but I know how snakes work.

(He didn't exactly say "you owe it to me" but it was close enough.)

my skin cells

will never forget the grip your hands had on them.

the way your nails dug into their soft spots.

they still feel the heat of your voice telling me

not to worry.

telling me to be still

and grateful

that a man wants to hold me this way.

this dirty, violent way.

they will not forget,

and I will not forgive.

I've crept into a concrete corner and crowned Anxiety as my king. The kind of royalty you want to overthrow but find yourself powerless against. I let him keep me there in his cage, and darkness blankets me.

Most days I find myself clasping my fingers together in prayer for the light to again find me. A savior to pull me out of Anxiety's sharp teeth. And sometimes the light shines at the edges of my shoes and I grab her hand to safety.

But I would be lying if I said there are never times when the light reaches out and I don't reach back.

How do you win a battle when you are both the <u>enemy</u> and the <u>ally</u>? The hurter and the healer? The one holding the trigger? Bullets ricochet in my rib cage.

I want to protect my land but I can't help but set fires to it. I don't mean to light matches but if I'm being honest,

> sometimes I like the burn
> sometimes I like the war
> sometimes I break my own heart
>
> and sometimes I want it to break more.

trying to run away and stay in the same place
wanting to continue but needing a break
aching for air but holding my breath
always wondering what's next
am i supposed to be here?
is this the right way?
afraid of decisions and of deciding too late
trying to find myself but always feeling l o s t
and each day that passes
the deeper i'm drawn

I collect every one of your fallen eyelashes on the pillow next to me when you sleep in this little jar so if you ever leave me I'll have plenty of wishes to bring you back home.

I am terrified of your love because
      he said the same things,
      he felt the same way
at some point
and then in the end,
      he left.
I am scared you might do the same
without realizing it.

I am absolutely

<u>terrified</u>

of the way you make me

<u>feel</u>.

Sometimes it's easier to sew red flags into you than know none exist,

because I thought I could do anything.

I could love you in distance.

Yes, at first it was easy,

but soon each mile marker had me drained.

957, 958, is the distance to blame?

Maybe I'm missing something from you?

Perhaps a flaw I didn't see before?

I'll make up stories in my head of why of you I am not sure.

I don't know why I do it. I've tried to stop my hands from stitching, sewing "DANGER! DANGER! Turn around!" into every daydream.

You are one without red flags or any flaws that matter.

I need to keep reminding myself this and let the plane rides pass in blurs.

Though my mind distorts my view of you from time to time,

forever I will choose to remain color-blind.

I live in half sentences

     half apologies

     half commitments.

I've never known how to be someone who lives in full.

I'm scared of all this empty.

And so, as a fair warning, a road sign telling you to be cautious down this path, I asked:

"What if I can only give you a half love?"

You took my shaky hands and held them.

"If I am lucky enough to experience half of your love,

     that is more than enough."

When you know the end is nearing the horizon but choose
to look the other way (because how do you say what's
already been said by thick silence?),

it's like feeling broken bones before they have been broken.

Living a life with bold lips that turn soft-spoken.

A burnt-out heart that's been awoken yet all along knowing:

This is not forever.

There will come an end.

The past clouds your vision. Pools into your eyes. And I take the shape of her, only for a few seconds. And for all the days we've moved forward, it takes such little time for us to move twice as far back.

(How many times do I have to say "I love you and I mean it" for you to realize? I. Am. Not. Her.)

loving and leaving you both feel like a mistake.

i'm trying to make the right one.

I am sorry for all the endless talks about my fears and insecurities. I need extra reassurance because I've never met someone I've wanted more, and this wanting could ruin me.

When my heart picks up and starts beating a million times
per second,

will you be the one to kiss it to sleep?

What if your mind
changes as quickly as
the color of your eyes,
and you decide
you no longer love me?

I've never been as scared to lose a love as I am of losing yours.
Every time your fingertips graze my skin,
my heart fills with fear.

Fear of losing that touch.
Fear of it being the last.
Fear of falling in love
and not being loved back.

I am
addicted to
&
terrified of
my own sadness

What if you grow tired?
What if one day
you sit down at breakfast
and I see dark circles pooling beneath your eyes
and I ask about them?

You might say you didn't sleep well,
although I didn't feel you tossing and turning.

Maybe that one sleepless night turns into many
and each morning, the circles darken
until finally
Tired is done sneaking up on you
and hits you at full force.
And maybe then,
maybe then I won't ever feel you toss and turn again.
I won't ever be with you again.

Every night, I pray you won't grow tired of me.

I can sense the fear in your eyes. It washes up behind you and pulls you under. How beautiful the ocean of you, how dangerous she can be, leaving you stranded on an island of your own thoughts. How lonely. Survival will only be for those who are the strongest swimmers. Those who are the strongest willed. Able to open their eyes under water despite the salt and toxicity. And keep them open when they see sharks circling under their feet. Those able to push past fear's immobility and move forward.

Continue on, my love.

Keep swimming.

AND WHEN THE STORMS ROLL IN AS THEY ALWAYS
DO,

I WILL BE YOUR UMBRELLA.

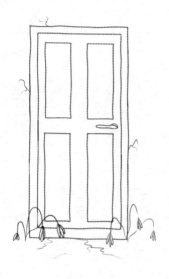

ROOM #3 - IN HEARTBREAK

Oh, you've been heartbroken?
Welcome to the Poets' Club.
Beware: it's a sad place.

The stars fell to dust and the colors melted to dust and my fingertips turned to dust the second yours waved goodbye.

I didn't invite heartbreak into my home but as some of us know, it doesn't knock or ask to come in.

It breaks down doors.

It shatters windows. It smashes walls.

It finds its way into every picture frame and the sheets of the bed.

Every meal, every dream, each time I look at the coat rack and see only one jacket hanging.

There is no good way to leave someone.

But to leave silently, with questions left unanswered on the welcome mat and the promise of forever returned like a spare key . . .

that's the cruelest way to leave.

My demons have returned.
One for every time I say
        I miss you
to the empty space next to me.
One for each time I've cried.
Another for every nightmare
that you are here and decide to leave me.
I guess that's my reality.
You chased them away
with that smile of yours
and the gentle touch of your sweet words,
but here they are again,
resting on my shoulder
as I chase after you.

i wish forgetting you
were as easy as
rolling through a car wash
and coming out clean of your name

I've been trying for so long to give myself to you.

Isn't that what you are supposed to do for the ones you care about most? Give them parts of you to hold?

I want you to open your palms toward me

so I can cradle myself between them,

but you walk around with closed fists.

It's like trying to make a color-blind man understand the color red.

You can't make a loveless man understand love.

Like a creeping fog crawling over a creek, seemingly harmless and quiet but just as deadly, the silence that has fallen will be what leads us to goodbye.

You don't know it's coming but once it's there, the deal is done. Thick and heavy, a war has been won. Even when we are fighting on the same team, still, indifference has forced us to our knees and made us known to empty forevers.

I'd say *I miss you* but I don't know how.
You'd say *Don't leave* but you're too proud to admit that we were both wrong.

This isn't what I wanted, but we got it anyway.

SPRING CLEANING

time to wipe down counters / to donate old, worn clothes /
to donate your faded grey hoodie i've held on to for three
years / to dump the perfume you bought me in the sink / to
throw away our box of memories / to unhang your ghost in
my closet that i've kept around on lonely nights / to wipe
your shadow from the walls / your scent from my bed / the
memory of your touch from my fingertips / to brush my
tongue until it no longer holds the syllables of your name

I like messy.

I like chaotic.

I just don't like a mess being made out of me.

You enjoy ripping my heart at its seams, don't you? The corners of your lips turn upward at every crushing goodbye. It must be a game to you. Play me once, play me twice, how many different ways can you break me before I'm nothing but a spine?

I thought maybe this time was different. (How naive of me to think things could be different.)

This is me cutting ties. I sent you this poem so you could read it and know, I'm no longer a name you get to hold between your teeth.

But still,

I'm sure you'll rip the spine of this book just to break me in another kind of way.

I'm twenty-one and I've outgrown playgrounds,
but last week I found myself lining up the edges of a piece
of paper, making a fortune teller like I would in third
grade, and sliding my thumbs and index fingers into their
respective slots. I counted to myself, "1, 2, 3, 4." Open, close,
open, close.

Pretending I didn't already know the destiny I'd made.

Pretending underneath every flap I hadn't written your
name.

The problem with being a poet is

everything is a metaphor.

So when they tell you they love you, you paint it grander than it is.

And when they tell you goodbye, it hurts more than it should.

The rivers flow into the sea, which I can't help but think of as a metaphor for you and me.

I'm always running back to you, pouring myself into you, thinking if I can just give you a little more this time, you will finally be able to love me the way I've wanted.

You wild thing.
Always cold and reckless.
Always unforgiving, drowning sailors in your beauty.
You almost got me.
      Perhaps you still will.

I promise someday I will be the ocean.
I will be the ocean.
I will be the ocean.

(Right now I am still your river and I am both relieved and greatly ashamed.)

I knew the brakes didn't work
but still I chose to get in the car.
Mind clouded by immediate wants,
not thinking of the disaster this would cause.
Now I'm bracing for the crash,
wishing that the first time you asked
I hadn't chosen to take your hand.

I'm looking in a mirror and I see you everywhere.

The reflection of my eyes holds you in them. You're trapped there.

My hands are stained with the memories of holding yours.

My hair is unbrushed and falls haphazardly around my face, which reminds me of the messy way you left me.

I miss you in myself.

I don't need to wear black for everyone to see I am mourning the loss of your love.

I turned twenty-one today.

And you didn't wish me a happy birthday. I knew it wouldn't be a forever thing, but I thought I'd make it to thirty before you'd stop texting. Maybe you have new birthdays to celebrate.

I bought a cupcake and a candle at Maggie's and quietly sang to myself in my kitchen. And then blew out the flame with one breath.

I know I'm not supposed to tell you what I wished for but I will say

it looks a lot like your hand in mine.

It looks a lot like you staying.

I pick up a shell and I hear you. Your voice still carries in the wind. Is this you calling out to me? You've always been my ocean. The arms I run to, to refresh and find my calm. Now every shell I listen to echoes either the hollow goodbye you left me with or the crashing of waves in my heart at your memory.

Either leaves me broken.

you pick fights
like you're picking up groceries.
a casual, weekly thing.
i'm always wondering
what's on your list,
down which aisle you'll turn,
what you will buy into
and what you'll return.

i hope it's not my love,
but then sometimes i hope it is.

I saw a slug bug on the way home and had no one to punch. I even reached over, fist clenched, to the passenger seat out of habit. My hand isn't used to you being gone.

The ride home was lonely without you singing songs next to me. I turned on a playlist called "Summer Vibes" to keep myself from crying, but even the happiest of songs turn sad in your absence.

I miss you everywhere already.

And then I got home and saw the bed was still a mess where you had slept next to me the night before, and it broke me.

I lay on your side of the bed and held myself the way you would if you were here.

I miss you.

I miss you.

The time we had wasn't enough.

A whole lifetime wouldn't be enough.

Maybe broken is beautiful.

Maybe the abstractness of all my pieces shattered on the floor will lure in critics from afar as they give me 5 out of 5 stars and say, "How did you create such a masterpiece?"

And I'll answer:

"It was an accident of self-destruction."

You put the needle in its track.
Our hearts beat fast to a new romance.
In rhythm across the living room we moved
but as the song ended, I think we both knew
that I was the only one falling.

I guess in love you win and you lose
but with you,
I lost everything.

I met a man at a bar where I never should have been. He reminded me a lot of you. The version of you when we first met. The one that still exists kindly in my mind.

"You from around here?"

I told him no. I didn't want to be associated with a town that has known your name.

He offered to buy me a vodka cran. I told him I'd take whiskey.

"Trying to forget someone?"

Yeah, something like that.

"I take it you know a thing or two about love then."

What do I know?

Your hands, and endings, half-hearted apologies, wheels turning away from my porch, closure being a foreign word. I know the song of slamming doors. I know war cries and red lights that stay red and red flags that deepen. I know cardboard boxes and phone calls at 2 a.m. Dirty sheets, empty kisses, fortunes in cookies I pray come true. I know silent dinners, chewing our love with regret, calling it love when I know it wasn't.

"All I know is it all ends in heartbreak."

I downed the whiskey and left.

somewhere
there's life in me
but it's buried
underneath
all the memories
of us

But what if you keep waiting and I don't return?

What if I move on with a new lover?

What if I just don't love you anymore?

He replied, "For you, I'll always be waiting."

And my heart broke in a way it hadn't before.

He has a way
of summoning all the rain
and leaving it to pour over my house.
The storms follow me around
because of his leaving.

I'll continue to chase sunsets
and rainbows
and shooting stars.
I'll chase everything beautiful,
including your heart,
even if I may never reach it.

(Honestly, I'll spend my whole life
chasing you.)

losing you feels like
        falling
and   falling
and   falling,
an eternal dropping through the wind.
nothing to stop me,
nowhere to land
to end my heartache.

I miss you all over.

In places I didn't even know I could miss you.

Sure, I miss you with my hands and my heart,

but what surprises me

is the missing you in songs and swings at the park and in
the grass that glimmers underneath the sunsets we watched.

The heavens are angry.

The angels are crying

as we gather here, faces lit by burning-out candles.

Maybe it is him, already crowned and sobbing for the river his parents made, the ocean of his brothers.

He creates a monsoon.

"I am here! I am here!"

But all we hear is thunder and the deafening silence grief brings.

—Homage to a boy taken from us too soon

the rope is held by one last string.
it's me, both arms outstretched,
being pulled in different directions,
surprised i haven't split in two.
the keeper of relationships,
the keeper of the truth.
but there will come a day
when i will have to leave
and then what will you do?
be two ends of a rope that once was,
lying side by side in a bed
that neither wants to be in,
a love story that dried up and rotted?
i can't be responsible for mending this.

He's leaving again.

I knew he wouldn't stay,

but I'd hoped for more time.

We always hope for more time.

There are no miles between us yet, but I already feel my heart being pulled far away, stationed in another country, beating for the both of us when I'm unsure if his is beating at all.

That's the worst part, the not knowing.

The unspoken.

The hearts and spirits broken.

He comes into view and I see a hurting in his eyes.

The pain of a man who knows coming and going,

who says "I'll see you soon," all the while knowing

soon could be years, soon could be never.

I whisper, "Please don't go," selfishly.

He nods like he doesn't want to but puts on his vest anyway. Ties his boots anyway.

He says,

    "I'll be back."

I nod knowing this is a prayer, not a promise.

You took all the birds with you as you walked out of my life,
and now who's to sing to me in the morning except the drumbeat of the lonely rain?

Is heartbreak inevitable?

Yes.

But I'd rather my heart break at the sound of your last breath than the sound of your goodbye.

The kindest thing to do now
would be to leave on your own terms
because we both know I won't.

We've always had a half-baked love.

One that smells nice from two rooms over

but falls apart the instant you try to hold it in your hand.

What if I erased the ending?

Rubbed away our last few pages?

So that the next person who reads our story only knows us in our Good and never in our Goodbye.

this will be my last poem about you. this will be my last
poem about you. this will be my last poem about you. this
will be my last poem about you. this will be my last poem
about you. this will be my last poem about you. this will be
my last poem about you. this will be my last poem about
you. this will be my last poem about you. this will be my
last poem about you. this will be my last poem about you.
this will be my last poem about you. this will be my last
poem about you. this will be my last poem about you. this
will be my last poem about you. this will be my last poem
about you. this will be my last poem about you. this will be
my last poem about you. this will be my last poem about
you. this will be my last poem about you. this will be my
last poem about you. this will be my last poem about you.
this will be my last poem about you. this will be my last
poem about you. this will be my last poem about you. this
will be my last poem about you. this will be my last poem
about you. this will be my last poem about you. this will be
my last poem about you. this will be my last poem about
you. this will be my last poem about you. this will be my
last poem about you. this will be my last poem about you.
this will be my last poem about you. this will be my last
poem about you. this will be my last poem about you. this
will be my last poem about you. this will be my last poem
about you. this will be my last poem about you. this will be
my last poem about you. this will be my last poem about
you. this will be my last poem about you. this will be my
last

an empty love will leave you broken;
your mind won't stop holding words unspoken.
a hand unknown to the warmth of another
will leave you colder than the harshest winter.
a life of solitude can be lonely.
to fall out of love will hurt you slowly.
looking in the eyes of a lover and seeing defeat
will leave an aching vacancy between the sheets.
no matter what you do, how you love and choose not to,
what you protect and what you don't,
where you stay and where you go,
a broken heart,
i promise,
you'll always know.

ROOM #4 - IN NOSTALGIA

The closet seems empty.

To the naked eye, it is.

But those who have lost, who have known the pain of a goodbye, they see the lining of ghosts draped from plastic hangers,

hung up because they are too loved to be thrown out but hurt too much to be displayed.

We keep them hidden, these dead romances, only to visit them when we are alone and lonely—two very different things, but together they create an aching emptiness we attempt to fill by opening this closet and dancing with these ghosts of the past, just for the night.

IF I COULD MAKE A HOME OF YESTERDAY

I'd pull it back from the sky
and wrap it around my skin
like a blanket needed in winter.
Somewhere underneath
I'd find your hand resting,
waiting for my fingers to
trace their way back to yours.
And tomorrow would not exist.
And neither would the goodbye you left me with.

There is a cemetery in my mind and every gravestone bears your name.

These are the things I no longer wish to understand:

1. The earth is slowly dying because of how we treat it.
2. Cancer.
3. Christmas becomes more stressful and less magical the older you get.
4. Love is not always what it seems.
5. Loneliness is the loudest state of being.
6. People will leave you broken on the floor and blame the mess on you.

I watched the Tempe Town Lake bridge fall last Saturday, and I thought how beautiful it is to crumble instead of burn. To have remains, a spine of memories, still in reach instead of ash that slips through fingers.

I wish our end could have been more like that, to have something to dig up. But here we are, familiar strangers, as if nothing ever happened.

I won't say I miss you, because it reminds me that there is something to miss.

and it's been a long while and I've been busy living a life full of color and zest, but there are times when I will be kissing a boy I just met and thinking of your name.

and there are times when my mind wanders off to think how this wonderful life might have been even better had you decided to stay.

If you knew I was a writer, would you still have taken my hand to dance? If you knew I would one day write about you, would you still have asked what song had changed my life forever? You always said you could tell a lot about a person based on the music they listened to. Maybe I should have listened more closely. Would you still ask me to stay over? Would you have kissed me softer? Said I love you more like a promise and less like a transaction? Would you have stayed instead of saying goodbye in passing? If you knew I'd paint you between these lines and only tell the truth and express the once beautiful, now deadly storm of you so that everyone after me would know how to weather your name, would you still have left me so damaged?

(I answered *"Lost in My Mind,"* but now when someone asks me what song has changed my life I always say your name.)

Sometimes people are meant to cross paths.

I know we were.

But that doesn't mean cross and then change course.

It doesn't always mean travel together.

For a while I took your hand.

But I think we both knew from the start

that this wasn't forever.

Maybe someday you'll marry someone else.
And maybe I'll be invited.
Maybe I won't.

Either way I'll hear about it.
And I'll be happy you're happy,
but that same wound will open up like a blooming flower,
and the pain of losing you will resurface again.

I'll write a third book about you
and you'll probably read it like the others

and still, that won't be enough to bring you home.

A nightmare I'm addicted to,
always,
I'll be loving you.

when did

vacuuming our living-room rug and scraping the
last of the ice cream out of the bowl

become the loudest part of our relationship?

Every time the song ends you die again.

You'll die a million deaths in my mind.

Every time I remember you, I also remember how badly I lost you.

The problem with me is
I always choose to see
what could be,
not what is.
My mother told me it's beautiful I see light in dark places,
but I've named it a curse.

Time and time again, it keeps me hoping we will work.

Even when I was falling into your Hell,
where promises burned and your "I love yous"
burst into smoke,

I thought,

"I'm sure there is someplace in here flowers could grow."

Even while you dream, I hope I cross your mind every once in a while. I hope you smile in your sleep at the sight of me. I hope you'll chase after me into whatever scene you've imagined. I hope your hand reaches out to mine and in that hovering moment before fingertips touch, I'll slip out of your dream.

But when you wake with a start from the sudden loss of me,

I hope you always know I'm only one call away.

My blood runs the same.
I'm still the girl in your frames,
but my hand navigates
to long brown hair
and the skin of women.

You loved me when my lips
had gone untouched by hers,
but men's lips don't taste like roses
or make me feel quite as alive.

This has always been a truth of mine.
One I've been trying to tell since packed lunches
and school-bus rides.
You chose not to listen.

You are still choosing not to listen.

But I can't keep waiting for an approval that will never
come.

I'm going back
to my roots
so I can again find
the words that have
been in hiding.

So then one day your name casually popped up in conversation and I blinked and my breath tripped, but only for a passing moment and then I was fine.

I don't stop breathing anymore. My heart doesn't skip and my airways don't close off and I'm not stuck reaching for air through a blanket of suffocating memories.

But your name still gives me a start.

I think it always will.

Some may call me foolish. Some may say I'm naive. But I don't regret a single thing.

I was a girl in love and willing to hold fire in my hands to make us work.

Sure, I have burns. But these are proof that I tried my best for what I wanted most.

I only ever gave up when the last match was lit and extinguished.

I only ever gave up when I had nothing left.

IN A WORLD WHERE THE WORDS "I MISS YOU" DON'T
EXIST, I SAY:
inspired by Caitlin Conlon

i wrote another poem about you / i punched the empty
passenger seat when i saw a slug bug / can you send me
your scent in an envelope? / i wore your old t-shirt to bed /
and the next day without washing it / when's the next plane
coming to seattle with you in it? / i go to an amusement
park and think, "C would have liked this" / i take mental
notes to take you back to every place i've been without
you, just so you can experience it / i say i love you over the
phone with a slight lull at the end / we both feel a pang
somewhere deep as we hang up and fall into empty beds

ROOM #5 - IN LOVE

"What's the most promising emotion?"

"What's the most destructive?"

For both I answered,

      love.

You started forest fires beneath my skin.

Flames flooded my veins.

The worst part is,

I liked the burn.

Even when it was

      d e s t r o y i n g

me.

I want to write you a beautiful poem as tribute to all the good you give me. One that carries as much light as you do walking into a room.

When I think of you, I think of the sun and the moon kissing. You as a child born from their affairs.

You always bring me balance.

You always bring me hope.

The speed at which you split me open, found my vulnerable, and cupped it gently in your hand, it must have been unprecedented.

But it feels safe there.

Your palms were meant to be home to the most delicate parts of me.

I used to think I wouldn't find a love that fit.

But you came along and opened a soft spot inside of me, and I've kept your name tucked in that same spot ever since.

A warrior believes the next battle will be won, no matter how many defeats he's faced.

I am a warrior of love.

Little details are slipping from my lips.

Things I never thought I would say.

You are pulling them out with every kiss.

I hope you are one who stays.

You are making me smile for no other reason than the thought of yours.

Thank you for allowing me space for myself. I've met men that have tried to suffocate me. Men that have tried to put me in a box. Men that have tried to drain me of my words and make me lose myself within the abyss of them.

You are my abyss of never-ending curiosity and love, but you don't let me get lost in it. I know you. I love you. There's still more to learn. But you remind me that you are meant to be next to me, not to enfold me. That I stand on my own and if I trip you'll be there to catch me, but you believe in my strength to stand again.

I have a voice and you don't muffle it. You pour gasoline on it, as if my ideas are meant to be ignited, my words are supposed to be heard. You embellish my creative side and ask for more without ever asking for too much.

I know who I am when I am with you and when I am without you.

You have taught me it is okay to take up space, and that I am beautiful for doing so.

I must have known you in another lifetime, because everything about you is so familiar.

I'VE BEEN IN LOVE BEFORE,
BUT NOT LIKE <u>THIS</u>.
NOTHING IN THE WHOLE WORLD
HAS EVER BEEN LIKE <u>THIS</u>.

if you could cut me open
i'm sure you would find
a whole museum of every word
you've ever spoken to me

. . . and, heartbreak after heartbreak, my life ran into you. I told myself I wouldn't let you have my heart, because i was convinced you would only break it like every person before, but you stayed put and wouldn't leave without it. Hesitantly, I handed it over. I still don't know if it was to shut you up or because I truly did want to, despite how terrified I was. I watched you day and night, eyes always glancing toward your hands, making sure my heart was still there and not abandoned. Every time I looked, it was. You held it, cared for it, fed it the love it had been yearning for for so long. With every new sunrise you taught me that I am worthy and deserving of an unconditional love.

i fell in love like it was just another errand to run

I see the entire world beneath your skin.

Your eyes are the color of the ocean.

The goosebumps I leave are all the mountain ranges.

All the world's most beautiful monuments lie within your kiss.

I don't need to buy a plane ticket to see all that I could ever want to see.

All I need is you.

Come sleep in my heart.
Make a home of it there.

your lips draw out my hesitancies.
kissing you makes me Brave,
like i could fight off rainstorms
and battle my inner wars
and come out unscathed.

You have dreams that go beyond me and I can't bear to hold you back, no matter how much you say I'm more important and no matter how much I love you. I think letting you go is the greatest act of love I will ever commit. You deserve to hold your dreams in your hands and not in your head. With me here, you'll never reach out to them.

So I'm going to break my own heart and let you go, my love, because it's what's best for you.

Sometimes love is doing what's worst for me.

You are the sun that warms my lips
and the moon that cradles me at night.
A new star forms with every kiss.
You are every light in my life.

I'll walk to you.

If the car doesn't start and the plane is delayed, the train cancelled and the bus is late.

If all the damn horses in the world run away.

I will walk all 1,090 miles

      if it means I get to be next to you.

If you lie next to me at night
and the moon blinks away
and the stars hide behind the darkness,
I'm glad to know I'll still have light
with every one of your kisses.

I've built these walls to withstand
every flirty glance,
each quick comment,
any chance of heartbreaking romance,
and they have for several men.
But somehow you,
you found a way to make them
all
fall
down.

You shouldn't fall in love with me.
I'll turn you into poetry
and leave you lying here between these lines
forever.

This probably won't last,
but I've been broken
time and time again
and I'm pretty good
at putting myself
back together by now
so, go ahead, have my heart.
I'll take that chance.

WHEN OUR TIME EXPIRES
MY LOVE FOR YOU WON'T

Things I never told you:

1. The only reason I went on the first date is because my previous plans had been cancelled and I didn't want to spend the night alone.

2. You gave me many reasons to go on the second.

3. I never really liked your sister.

4. Every time I replied "stop it" when you called me beautiful, I most definitely did not want you to stop.

5. The color blue has now become my favorite color.

6. The smell of your mom's quiche is the smell I look most forward to every year.

7. When you whispered "I love you" and I didn't say it back, I wanted to.

8. But I was scared.

9. I'm terrified of love and what it could do to me.

10. I'm terrified of you and your ability to ruin me.

11. But still, here I am falling.

You are the reason the sun rises and the moon glows. The universe could not handle keeping your beauty hidden in the dark, even for a moment.

You are a work of art to be known.

You come with baggage.
But I've decided
I'll be okay carrying a few extra bags
for the rest of my life.

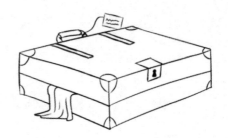

The silence that rests between us is comfortable. It's not heavy or overbearing. It's a light presence in the air. A family kind of silence. I always knew you were family.

I want to tell you things I've never told anyone before.

I want to show you my entire world.

I want to open myself up, let all my walls fall down, let all my insecurities fall away.

I want to let you all the way in.

You make me want to be <u>vulnerable</u>.

I adore all of these stolen moments with you.

Your kiss is pulling all of my deepest fears out of the darkest parts of my belly. The weight of them floats into the air. You are making me feel light again. Like I did before I was old enough to be hurt by people.

Stop wondering if your body takes up too much space in a room.

Even more, stop wondering if your words do.

I don't know if there is a god
but every night I pray
that it's you + me
at the end of this.
At the end of the world
I want to be holding your hand.

I am sitting on a plane and I want to write you a letter, because the way the sun hit the water as we slid up into the sky reminded me of the glimmer in your eyes when you see me smile.

As we fly further up, the people become tiny ants and the cars remind me of the Hot Wheels I played with as a child. And I think how small and insignificant each of us is. Living our lives as if they are the only lives to live. As if there aren't billions of other tiny ants driving their tiny cars, living their tiny lives. It reminds me how vast this world is and how miniscule the scope of mine is. I feel so small.

But then I think of you. Your tiny, insignificant life and how it collided into mine. How it rippled the earth beneath our feet and created the largest earthquake known to man. Up here, that collision can't be seen. But we felt it. We felt it rattle our cores and completely disrupt our lives' paths. I don't care how small we are or that we drive little Hot Wheels cars.

That.

That catastrophic collision and that feeling in my chest.

That has to be significant.

can you whisper every thought to me?
i want to hear them all.
i could spend hours under
the hypnosis of your voice.
oh what i would do to spend a lifetime.

For all the things I write down on paper
there are thousands of words I have yet to say.
It is easy for me to show my fear
because it has a name.
Sadness appears in all my books
because for each of us, tears fall the same.
But the love I have for you,
that's difficult to write
because for all the words I know,
yours I can't seem to find.
Nothing amounts to how beautiful you are.
How gentle, loving, and kind.
I could spend years staring at an empty page
because no alphabet, word, or language to describe you
would suffice.

ROOM #6 - IN HOPE

This is me reclaiming my name.

Pulling it out of the teeth of those who have hurt me.

Taking back my part in my own damn play.

I'm the main character and this is <u>my story</u>

and it doesn't start with others' hands around my neck.

It starts HERE.

This is my beginning.

Hold on to hope.

Even when it pulls you underwater to the deepest depths of the ocean on a tight leash that forces you to hold the breath you never got to catch,

HOLD ON.

I've become broken
but my heart beats.
I've shattered the mirror
but I still see me.
Though fraying and contorted,
I am and will always be
the spirit that's hurting
but finds strength to set herself free.

It's been almost three years and when I pass by your house on the walk to my mailbox, I'll admit I still look up. Wondering if I'll see your mom gardening on the front lawn. I'm always crossing my fingers in prayer that I do because I miss her most. But I'm never wishing for you. Or praying not to see you. I've found myself in neutrality. Where my glance at your window is only out of curiosity, not hunger or pain. I'm okay with your existence, and your leaving, and your existence after leaving. I'm better than okay.

I've moved on.

How to move on:

1. Know healing isn't linear and there is not one way to do it.

2. Get into bed and lie in the middle, take up all the space. You don't have to choose a side anymore.

3. Learn how to stop associating the word "love" with their hands.

4. Eat all the ice cream you please.

5. Write about it all.

6. Write, write, write.

When you look down
and see a mountain
laid across your belly,
your first thought
doesn't have to be:

"How do I conquer this?"

You should be proud
to hold nature's beauty
under your skin.
The earth is made of
hills and valleys;
it is never truly flat.

You shouldn't feel like you need to be, either.

This one's for me.

For all the times I've felt like I needed to be more. For all the times I've felt like I'm invisible. For all the late nights and bloodshot eyes that turn redder every hour I can't force myself to fall asleep. For the many years my heart belonged to a boy that didn't belong to me. For all the put-downs and all the terrible things my mind whispers quietly. About me. For all the wishes I dreamed to change my reality.

This one's for me,

to remember things get better despite how it may look.

The mirror will say you are flawed, but look into the reflection of my eyes and they will tell you that you are flawless.

I've been doing a lot of reflecting in all my time alone. And naturally I thought of you. I thought of us and everything I thought we were. I used to tell my sister you were magic. That I'd never met a man who could command a room the way you could. But now with years between conversations, I'm beginning to understand that I was looking at you through rose-colored glasses. That all magic is deception. You didn't command a room, you commanded my attention (and mine only). Everyone else heard your voice between all the others, while I had tunnel hearing.

Your final words hurt me.

"I don't love you anymore. I'm not sure if I ever did. I think I only loved the idea of you loving me, and I'm sorry for that."

It felt like a collision and I wasn't wearing my seat belt. I wasn't bracing myself. I wasn't prepared for an ending.

But they also brought me clarity, albeit years later.

I would have never been able to see you for who you really are, had you not cut me loose.

Thank you for doing what I never could.

Whatever's happening to you right now, these are the days this must happen.

Not later.

Not never.

Right. Now.

These days will shape you.

They may hurt you.

They will make you stronger.

They have to happen to make you who you are meant to be.

I can't wait until you meet her.

You give me hope like spring gives flowers.
Any rain that rolls in will only make us stronger,
and I believe beautiful things can bloom from this love.

love letter to the leaves

with all that's been happening, i've turned to dark places and i've hid there the past few days. i tend to do that. i know i need to stop, but that's for another time.

i took a walk outside today. i needed to be reminded that good things still exist. and there you were. growing, thriving, unchanged by the news that's been constantly breaking me. that keeps Anxiety knocking on my door.

i held you in my hands. i put you up to my nose. and i felt renewal climb up and down my spine.

the symbol of life.

today you reminded me that i am Alive

and that is something to celebrate.

yours,
      M

When we're young our minds, personalities, even bodies, can be manipulated. We are soft, pliable, unmolded. But as we grow up, we begin to collect these different parts of the world and glue them to our shells, forming a unique exterior. Instead of a blank slate, we create the art of who we are, even if we aren't artists.

I hope as you grow and continue to build your beautiful shell that you've learned to sprinkle kindness on it and that the pasted-on confetti represents both excitement and curiosity. I hope all the red marks are times you've been in love instead of times you've been in anger. I hope the paint splatters were done out of spontaneity and the water marks are from all the times you decided to jump into the ocean instead of holding back. I hope you got your hair wet and laughed. I hope all the windburns were from free-falling (in opportunity or love) and that they never hurt. I hope every rock you've picked up and stuck in a crevice demonstrates your strength for not breaking but healing all your cracks.

I hope by the end of this life your shell is heavy with passion and experience,

and not a day went by that you didn't add to it.

Go out.

Collect those stars.

Make those dreams come true.

The only person holding you back

is YOU.

Throughout the windstorms and the rain
you have stayed alight.
Throughout the hurting and heartbreak
you have stayed alive.
Know there is more hardship coming
but I believe in your fight.
When the dark days come again,
your fire within will be your light.

With you,

I am everything I've ever been told that I'm not.

ANXIETY AS A TROUBLESOME NEIGHBOR

She's always turning up on my welcome mat uninvited and has two feet through the door before I can say hello. It's always at the most inconvenient of times, and she will make me sit inside for hours before she leaves. Sometimes she doesn't leave for days.

I'm always nice and accommodating and offer her coffee and never interrupt her tangents, but I'm tired of being nice. I'M TIRED.

So, today,

I'll knock on her door, unexpected and proud, and tell her she cannot come over. That I have errands to run and I am way too busy for her company. That if she needs me, she can leave a voicemail but I WILL NOT ANSWER.

Not today.

The unspoken stains itself on blank pages. Movement of the hand is easier than saying it. Just getting it out there, down, done with so it doesn't burn in my veins any longer. But perhaps writing it is more courageous. I'll put all these unspoken words into a book and let the hands of thousands hold them.

Maybe they will find a home in one of them when they couldn't make a home of me.

No matter how many times I've been and will be hurt, all the times I've fallen and will fall again, I choose to believe despite all the bad that people are good.

That there will always be hands to help lift me from scraped knees, to hold on to in the dark, to soften a fall on concrete. That there will be eyes that light my way and comfort me whilst weathering my inner storms.

Evil exists in dark places but good always balances. Shine light and gather where darkness pools. Goodness is more powerful.

It's better to walk into the fire
than never feel the heat of the flames.

Because you can't shove darkness into a box and tape it shut and you can't flick it away either, you have to move yourself, your own two feet, in any direction (because there's really no way to tell which way is right, and is there even a right way?) and keep moving. Even if you're going in circles, even if your legs get tired, keep pushing yourself through and eventually you will find light.

A fresh rose grows in the empty spot you left behind in my heart. Though the lights went out and tears rolled down my face, a part of me knew this had to happen. That I deserve more than what you had to offer. So a flower grows in the dark despite no love and no sun, because it knows better days are definitely yet to come.

I invite you to a dinner party where I am the guest of honor, and you get to silently watch me rise up as they call my name, make my way to the stage, leaving a trail of flowers blooming in my wake. I'll be taller than you remember (confidence gives you a few inches) and I'll be glowing. The lights focused on me and all I have accomplished, all that I have grown, since you left.

Press your hand to the wall. Don't pull it away when the cold concrete shocks you or when the unforgiving nature of it doesn't budge an inch. You can do this. Every day move a little closer, push a little harder until it softens, caves, gives in to your weight and crashes to the ground, sending up a dust storm.

The walls you build can be brought down with patience and determination.

You make music simply with the color of your eyes
and the way your wrists move the wind.

Some days will be harder than others. Some days you'll have to fight to swim against rough currents or combat lions with bare fists; you'll have to keep climbing your mountains with ropes tied to your wrists. You'll have to understand where to go without a map to guide you. Learn how to see in the dark without the light of the moon.

The days can be long and difficult but you are a warrior.

Keep on with your fight.

Sometimes joy hides in forgotten places.

My jaw tells me to stop holding in apologies.
To spit out the "I love yous" and let him lie restfully.
He doesn't need to be locked. He can be an open door.

My hands tell me to stop thinking them empty.
Sometimes I don't get to hold what I want,
but instead I hold what I need.
And that is still hands that are full.

My heart tells me there is no bridge between her and my brain.

That I need to stop trying to cross something that is broken.

She tells me the brain is good for science and writing equations but knows nothing of love.

"Stop knocking on his door to ask if you are doing it right. He will always tell you it's wrong, because there is no definitive answer.

There is only feeling.

And only I can feel your way toward home."

I no longer need to be needed.

I have no room for ropes on my wrists anymore.

This is me

       u n t e t h e r e d.

Unbelonging to anyone but myself.

Finally,

       finally

I have learned.

I am my own hero.

YOUR VOICE IS THE MOST POWERFUL THING ABOUT YOU;

DON'T LET SOMEONE ELSE SILENCE IT.

I'm jumping off this bridge into the deep water below.

Taking a risk, free-falling into the unknown.

I'm not sure if the waves will cushion me or feel like breaking glass against my skin

but hurting or healing, this is where my life begins.

Staying safe for so long has kept me well and alive, but peering over a bridge can't be all there is to life?

I want to jump into rivers and let my hair flow wild.

Know the pain of a lover leaving me behind.

I want to know broken and test my strength to fix myself.

You can't appreciate the beauty of Heaven without having experienced Hell.

"Tread lightly,"

      she said.

But I wanted to pound the water with my fists.

Kick it into the air.

Make ripples that ran for miles.

To make my own waves

and have the oceans know *my name.*

The rivers and the roads all lead to bigger things.
Your path may seem narrow, but your time is coming.

Sometimes when you start to read a new book, you don't realize who the main character is at first. They hover in the background, in small details and quiet conversations. Only later do they make their importance known.

I think my story is a lot like that.

My past chapters all had me playing a minor part. I kept my eyes down, thoughts hushed, passions tamed. But as I keep reading and living and growing, I'm starting to realize this is MY story. That I make the rules.

I AM THE MAIN CHARACTER.

I would like to take this space to thank the following people:

Michelle Halket, James Debono, and Jessica Peirce for making this collection come to life.

Venla Saarinen for the beautiful illustrations.

As always, my family for supporting me in every aspect of my life.

And, of course, to you. Thank you for choosing this collection. Thank you for supporting my dreams. Thank you for reading my words and giving them a home to rest.

Thank you.

Makenzie Campbell grew up in the Pacific Northwest and has been expressing herself through poetry since grade school. Following the success of her two collections, *2am Thoughts* and *Nineteen*, her newest collection *Rooms of the Mind* is brought to life. Makenzie is currently pursuing a psychology degree at Washington State University. She has plans for more books in the future, but in the meantime she enjoys traveling the world, creating art, and drinking a nice cup of hot cocoa.

@makenzie.campbell.poetry

Did you feel anything while reading this collection?
Feel free to write to Makenzie here:
2amthoughtsbook@gmail.com

For business inquiries, email:
mcbusiness9@gmail.com